Pat's Online Chat
Friends forever

by Margaret McArthur

Illustrations by Bryan Jason Ynion (BJY)

First Published by

Text copyright @ Margaret McArthur
Illustrations copyright @ Margaret McArthur

All rights reserved. No part of this publication may be used or reproduced, stored or introduced into a retrieval system, or transmitted, in any form or by any means (electronic, mechanical, photocopying, recording or otherwise), without prior written permission of the publisher - except in case of brief quotations used in reviews and/or academic articles, in which case quotations are permitted.

Written by Margaret McArthur
Illustrated by Bryan Jason Ynion (BJY)
Layout by Carolyn Tonkin Design
Printed by Ingramspark

National Library of Australia
Cataloguing-in-Publication data:
Margaret McArthur 2019

ISBN
978-0-6484449-7-8 (Paperback)
978-0-6484449-3-0 (Hardback)

For children age 6-10
Subjects covered, cyberbullying, technology use, bystander effect.

First Edition

This publication contains ideas and opinions of the author and is a fictional story. It is intended as a resource for informing children on the dangers of group chat bullying. Educators are advised to read through the book before commencing delivery to the intended audience.

The author and publisher assume no responsibility for any liability, loss or risk, personal or otherwise, which is incurred consequently, directly or indirectly, of the use and application of any content of this book.

This book is dedicated to my daughter Demi, her persistence and resilience in life is inspirational.

One fine Sunday, Rob was with his friend Pat.
They ran through the trees, stalking a great big bat.

The great big bat had soared out of a tree.
"I got it", Pat shouted filled with glee.

Sent to group chat

Pat was thrilled with her image and wanted to share.
She created a group chat and sent it without a care.

Everyone from the class soon joined the group chat.
They all wanted more pics of the great big bat.

The next day at school, Pat told everyone of the trees.
How they tipped to the side and rustled in the breeze.

Then, someone joined the chat who wasn't nice to Pat.

That someone shared a nasty pic to the group chat.

It was Mean Maisie who sent something cruel.

The picture was of Pat covered in drool!

The image showed Pat with an altered body.

It was stretched, enlarged, and shaped rather oddly.

Pat said to Rob, "I'm not worried, I don't care."
Maisie felt powerful and continued to share.

Rob confronted Maisie. "You're a bully. This has to end!"

Maisie just laughed, shrugged and continued to send.

Pat started to become upset and couldn't take anymore.
In one picture she resembled a rat, and it hurt her to the core.

After school Rob told Pat, "Go tell your dad."
However, his reaction left her feeling rather sad.

He **screeched** in response, "Stand up for yourself!"
But she was a shy bot and couldn't stop it herself.

Maisie's messages got worse, every day there was a new one. Pat stopped hanging out with friends, she stopped having fun.

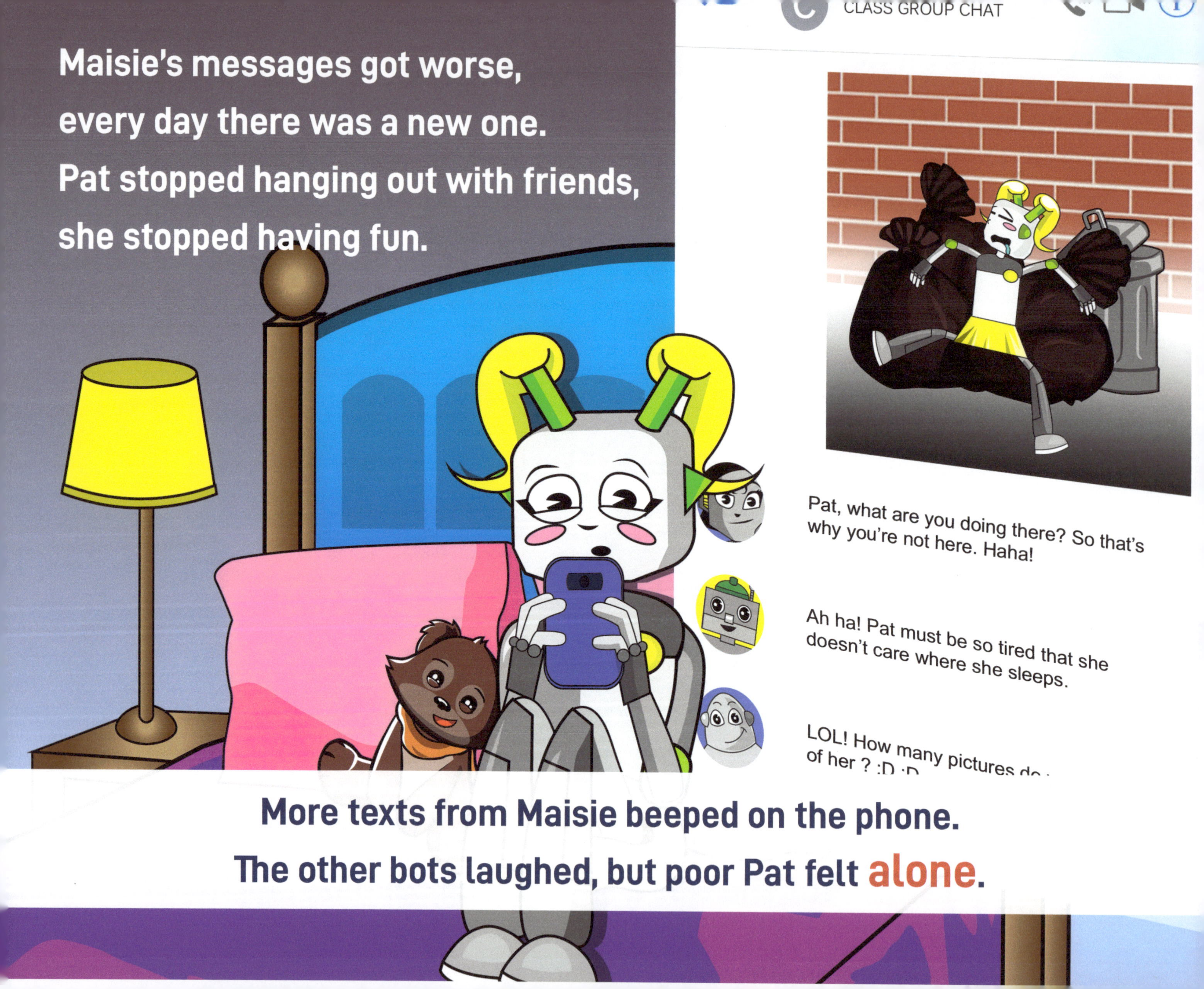

CLASS GROUP CHAT

Pat, what are you doing there? So that's why you're not here. Haha!

Ah ha! Pat must be so tired that she doesn't care where she sleeps.

LOL! How many pictures of her? :D :D

More texts from Maisie beeped on the phone.
The other bots laughed, but poor Pat felt **alone**.

Maisie printed some pictures and stuck them to the wall.

In the school yard, the images were seen by all.

Rob went to school and sat in his chair,
but Pat wasn't with him, she wasn't there.

The teacher Ms Smart, thought "Where could Pat be?"
On the phone Pat's mum said, "she's not with me."

Rob was really worried about his friend's absence.

He wanted to tell Ms Smart about the group chat madness.

Mean Maisie wouldn't stop, she wouldn't listen.
Rob felt **anxious**, he was afraid of the friction.

Panicked, Pat's parents searched everywhere for her.
They finally found her sitting with her older brother.

As they sat there together,
Pat revealed she felt lost.
She wanted to avoid school,
at any cost.

"I'm sorry" said Pat's dad. "I'm sorry I didn't act."

"I will fix this" he added. "I promise you that."

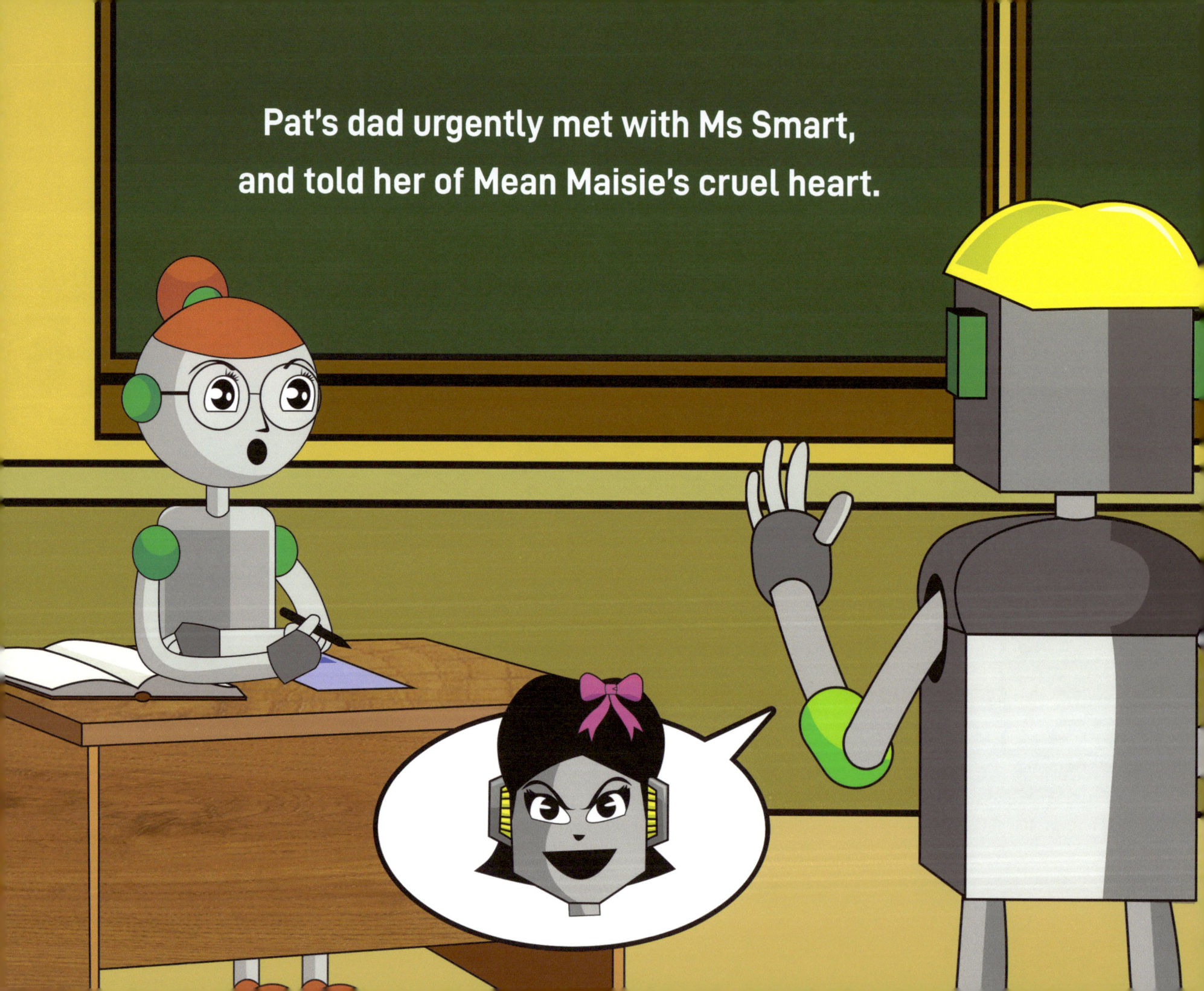

Maisie's bullying was now exposed and everyone knew.
She wept and she cried, she promised to start anew.

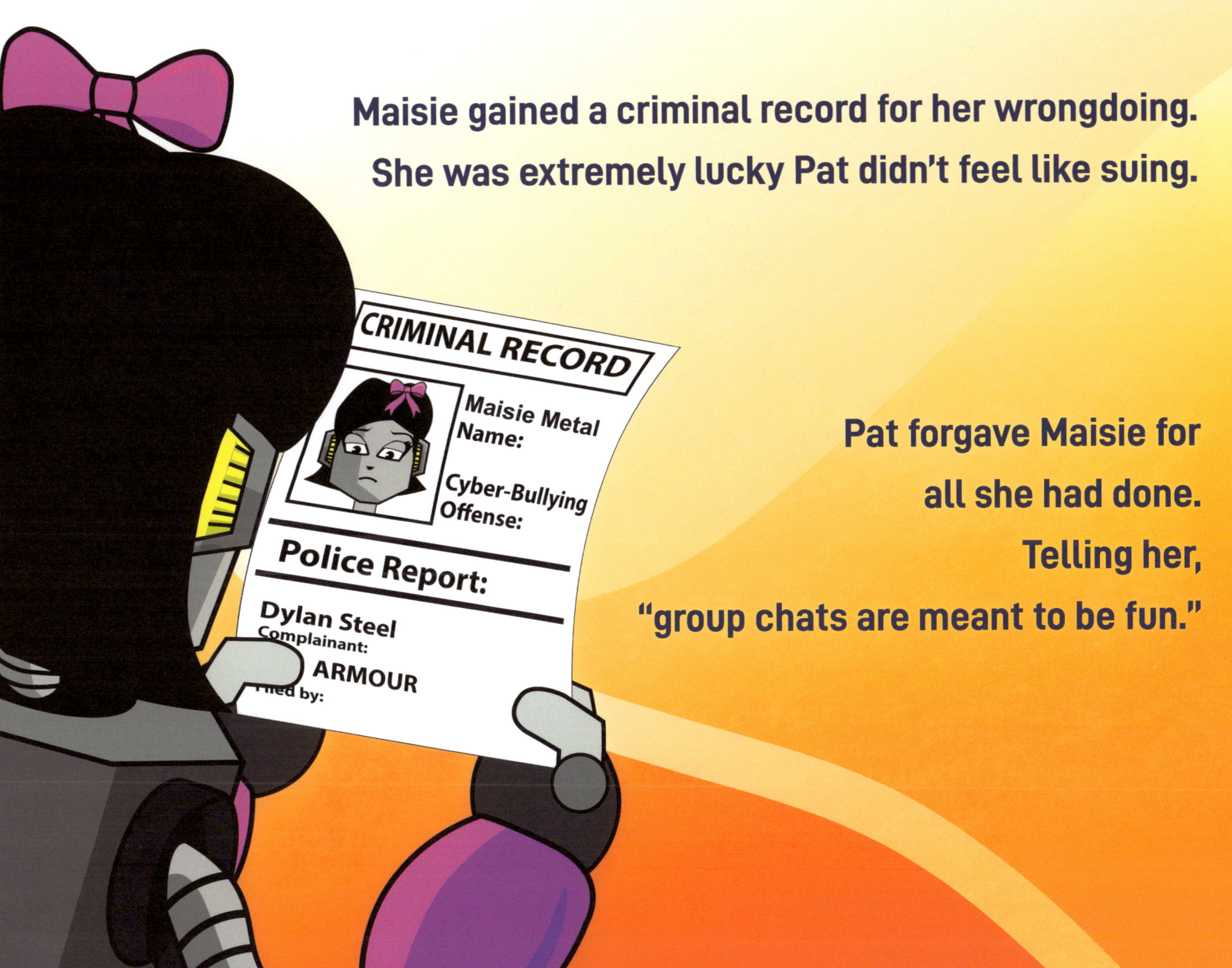

Maisie had learned her lesson, and suffered the **consequence**.
Pat returned to school, having regained her **confidence**.
The friends still enjoyed the group chat app,
they'd take pictures—pose, click, take a snap!

Rob was delighted, he had his friend back.
Pat was excited, she was back on track.

They made videos, dressed up and sang a rap.
They then sent it to the others still on the chat app.

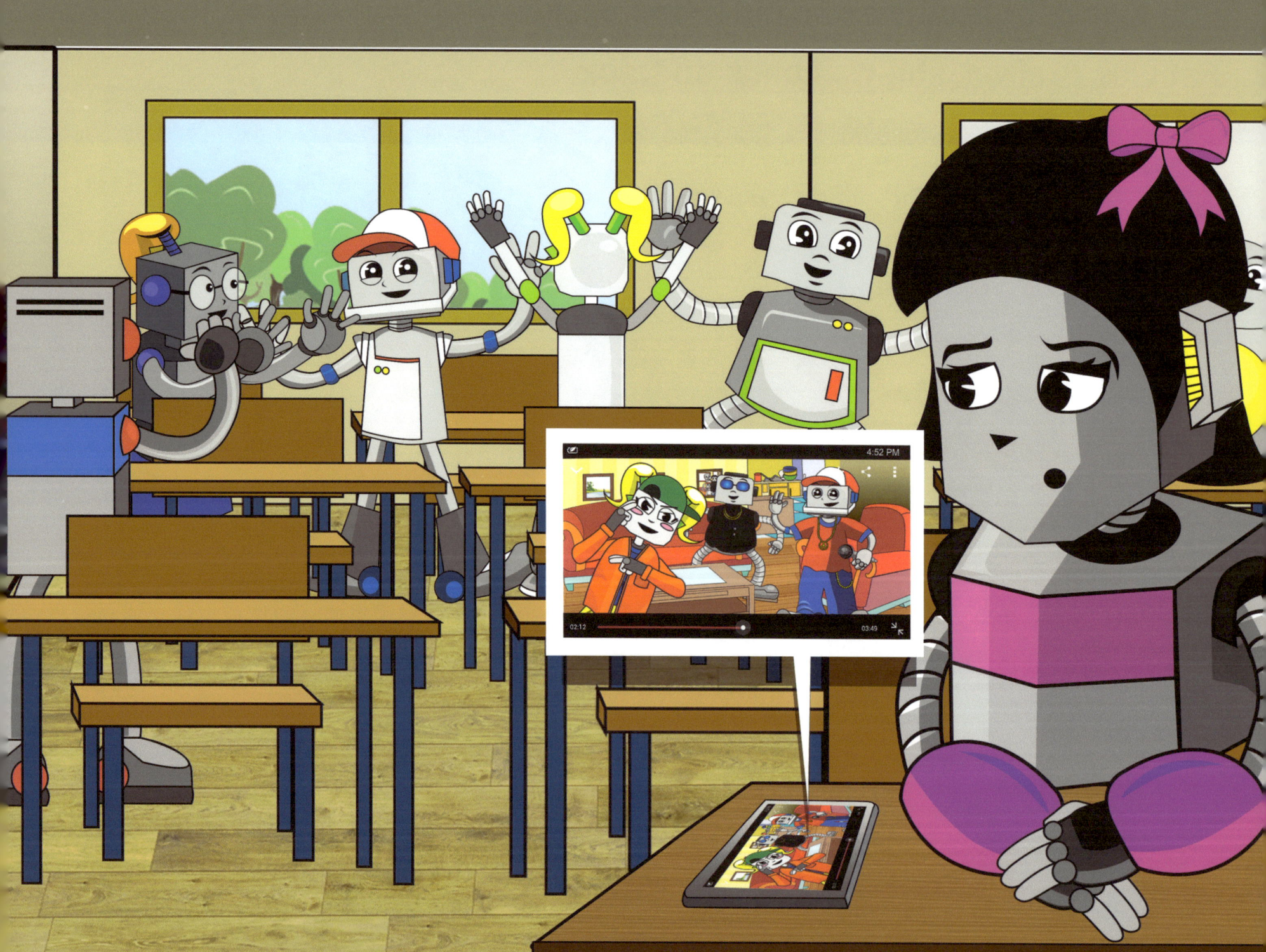

Mean Maisie saw the videos, she didn't laugh.

She didn't have a friend anymore, not even half.

The bots realised they engaged in the **'Bystander Effect'**.

From this day forward, their online motto is to

'PROTECT'.

Margaret McArthur is a teacher and leader of technology in Victoria. Since starting her teaching career in Scotland over a decade ago as a Secondary Computing teacher, she discovered a passion for eLearning, which encompassed the implementation and overview of the school Cyber Awareness program. The evolution of the program required early intervention of education in the younger year levels, due to the increased use of technology at an early age. With this increase of time online, children are more exposed to the pitfalls of the internet.

With education and support, our children can learn how to make informed decisions online as they learn to keep themselves safe in the real world. This led to the creation of her cyber safe books, addressing various aspects of online dangers to protect our children from external threats.

www.margaretmcarthur.com.au

www.ingramcontent.com/pod-product-compliance
Lightning Source LLC
Chambersburg PA
CBHW041326290426
44110CB00004B/154